Here We Com

D0105722

by Margie Sigman   illustrated by Nancy Speir

Harcourt

Orlando   Boston   Dallas   Chicago   San Diego

Visit *The Learning Site!*
www.harcourtschool.com

Copyright © by Harcourt, Inc.

All rights reserved. No part of this publication may be reproduced or transmitted in any form or by any means, electronic or mechanical, including photocopy, recording, or any information storage and retrieval system, without permission in writing from the publisher.

Requests for permission to make copies of any part of the work should be addressed to School Permissions and Copyrights, Harcourt, Inc., 6277 Sea Harbor Drive, Orlando, Florida 32887-6777. Fax: 407-345-2418.

HARCOURT and the Harcourt Logo are trademarks of Harcourt, Inc., registered in the United States of America and/or other jurisdictions.

Printed in China

ISBN 0-15-325477-7

10 121 10 09 08 07 06 05 04

Ordering Options
ISBN 0-15-325468-8 (Collection)
ISBN 0-15-326555-8 (package of 5)

We will go in a van.

We can not fit.

We will go in a bus.

We can not fit.

We will go in a cab.

We can not fit.

We can fit on a bike.
Here we come!